AMERICAN INJUSTICE

A MOMENT IN NORTH AMERICAN HISTORY

BY:

KELCEY S. GOODMAN

Copyright © 2020 Kelcey Shannon Goodman

All rights reserved

*Australia – Tjapukai Warrior
Aboriginal Cultural Festival*

<u>*Dedicated To*</u>

My Grandpa Shannon and all of us who supported and loved him

<u>*A Special Thanks To*</u>

All of those who understood

<u>*To Sterling Running Stream Phillips*</u>

For being an inspiration

American Injustice

What was once a serene co inhabitance between the Natives and what the land provided, vanished. Stripped of the right and pride to live peacefully amidst the natural world, a beautiful culture was driven out of existence. In the South Dakota Plains, renowned Indian Prairie, 1890, events occurred that were so odious they would be told throughout history then and even, still today. In the time and place of a cruel and horrifying massacre the Sioux Indians underwent one of the most heinous injustices of all time. Their tribe, like other Plains Indian of America carried on, through devastation and deprivation with what they could salvage.

There were many differences between the Natives and the settlers. There were differences that divided them apart. There were differences that collided. From the apparent superficial differences in appearance to the very evident cultural and lifestyle differences, people coming to America did not have enough *respect for those differences* or culture to try and live peacefully with them. The description written by Dee Brown tells us, "Now suddenly the trails were filled with wagons, and the wagons were filled with white

people" (8). There was a desire to attain what was not already in their possession and to own the land, gain wealth, and build New.

Some opinions were and still are that Natives of America were savage, immoral and bestial. This opinion would help, understandably, in any circumstance where the individual was attempting justification of what was, truly, the ultimate crime and injustice imposed upon the Natives. Many Indians saw the changes and modernization that the white people brought with them and agreed that they too should attempt to learn the new ways and develop some of the skill the newcomers had to offer. Several tribal leaders took initiative after befriending the white settlers to learn new ways of farming and raising livestock. Many carried that knowledge back to the tribe and encouraged them to learn the new way. Reported in an article of the Trail of Tears:

...were not nomadic savages. In fact, they had assimilated many European-style customs, including the wearing of gowns by Cherokee women. They built roads, schools and churches, had a system of representational government, and were farmers and cattle ranchers. A Cherokee alphabet the "Talking Leaves" was perfected by the Sequoyah (North Georgia).

North America was a goldmine for settlers. The land was an opportunity and their will was to create what they wanted to and make of the land what they wished, void of who was already there. There was no concern about the Native's culture. The Indians didn't have rights and weren't seen as people. They lived primitively and needed to be done away with according to the whites.

Those with money, power, and land had voting power and should be in control. There was no room for the culture and old ways of the Indians. They were viewed as heathens and there was a total conflict of beliefs. Fear of what they did not relate to, or want to try and understand, lead the way to hatred and an opinion that they were less than people. Natives did not understand ownership and therefore disagreed with selling their homeland, or even putting a price on it for that matter. Whites went to wicked measures to drive the Indians out.

One of the major food sources for the Natives was the buffalo. Often large herds were wiped out to starve the tribes through the winter. There was no appreciation nor consideration for their human rights and expression of culture. Settlers had their own agenda for America that did not include anyone who was already present. Chief Joseph of the Nez Perce had written in attempt to gain the understanding of the white people, "Perhaps you think the Creator sent you here to dispose of us as you see fit" (Brown). Questioning why they did not take care.

The Sioux possessed unmatched will, though no will of any form could withstand the pressure which would soon annihilate one of the most beloved people and ways of life to ever live free. Although the native people, marching to the beat of a primitive drum, held knowledge of unyielding value, they were berated, raped, and pillaged. Forced out of land they held sacred and into small, separated reservations where they were provided for what rations the government afforded them. However, it did not replace what they had taken, the

option to live as one, and to live bravely in harmony with their surroundings.

During the end of the fifteenth century, Natives had long welcomed travelers like Columbus and partook in trade and sharing. They learned new things from the people who arrived and taught the old way, how they "…lived from what nature provided in her bounty" (Dennis Banks 17). Soon the welcome was no longer appreciated, and as more and more Europeans arrived, the kindness ran out and wars waged. The Indians held their land as sacred and treated it as so. Twenty million Europeans, after robbing it of what they saw, squandered that land. The white man brought with them war, disease and alcohol. Tribes were driven westward and through the cold winters not many survived due to weather conditions, hunger, and disease.

The Indians struggled to find refuge in the Western Plain. "The killing, enslavement, and land theft had begun with the arrival of the Europeans. But it may have reached its nadir when it became federal policy under President (Andrew) Jackson" (North Georgia). Several of the Eastern tribes were moved out to reservations in the West. They were duped into selling their land for measly amounts and

were made promise after promise and none of them were kept. Except as one great warrior recalled, "they made us many promises, more than I can remember, but they never kept but one; they promised to take our land, and they took it" (Brown 449). In the eighteen thirties the discovery of gold made the land more sought after and staying, in peace, impossible for the Indians.

In the late eighteen seventies Indians had angrily left their reservations to meet with great warriors and fight for their lands. They had a couple of victories against the US Cavalry. The Sioux Indians were in luck and paired with great forces from the Cheyenne, would defeat the young and unprepared Colonel at the Battle of Little Bighorn. Custer was not knowledgeable of the surrounding landscape and would have to traverse through difficult terrain to make his assault. As the article tells, "Ignoring orders to wait, he decided to attack before they could alert the main party. He did not realize that the number of warriors in the village numbered three times his strength" (Eyewitness History 1). The tribes combining created a power that the Cavalry would not be able to defeat.

After the death of George Armstrong Custer in this battle, white onslaught reprised by placing the Black Hills outside the reservation boundaries and open for white settlement. Crazy Horse along with Sitting Bull and his warriors were broken and defeated. Though one of the most powerful and massive shows of Indian warrior bravery, the sacred lands continued to be taken, along with their heart. Crazy Horse was killed soon after in an attempted escape. In a

skirmish between Indian police, Chief Sitting Bull was accidentally shot.

Many Sioux were taken into a camp and four days after Christmas in eighteen ninety occurred the massacre at Wounded Knee. Like Custer's last stand, this was a slaughter, and many men died. There was something incredibly different about this incident. This time, possibly out of revenge, the Sioux were those who would pay the ultimate price. The Braves that fought in the battle at Little Bighorn fought to keep from being killed. In defense they fought against the US Cavalry's attack. The people killed at Wounded Knee were not armed. They had made no threat to attack the US soldiers, they were not hostile.

The Sioux had been attempting travel to Pine Ridge for safety. They were intercepted and brought to Wounded Knee camp and given rations. Fearful of a Sioux uprising, the following morning a call was ordered for the Indians to surrender their guns and arms. Many of the Indians had purchased their arms. The Indians surrendered their weapons and one, reluctant to give in, struggled and a gun fired. The US soldiers were fearful and the Natives' Ghost Dance was intimidating, "the Ghost Dance…revitalizing the Indians and bringing fear to the whites" (Eyewitness History 1). This set off the cavalry and indiscriminate+ slaying of every single one of the Indian prisoners commenced. Most of them were women and children.

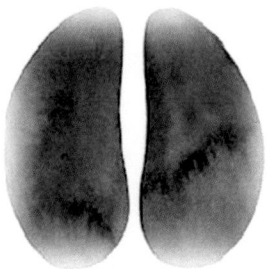

In the last quarter of the twentieth century again protests and stand offs continued in efforts to gain the respect and hope of some good to come out of all of the broken promises and misleading the American government handed the Indians. The American Indian Movement took form and several supporters paved the way to protest and draw attention to the hardships Native Americans today still faced. Many who lived on reservations were poverty stricken and lived miserable lives, many falling to alcoholism. During the events at the second Wounded Knee, several activists were killed. The Natives and supporters alike stood their ground and held strong for months on end.

The Militant Indians organized for action. Injustice was served and needed to be recognized. The Federal Government had broken hundreds of Indian Treaties and the Natives only hope was that the government would hold hearings on the Fort Laramie Treaty of eighteen sixty-eight. On Friday, May eighth, nineteen seventy-three, the final stand down occurred at Wounded Knee. AIM activists seized the South Dakota site and demanded the attention to the cause needed. This paramount event stemmed the examination of the treaty right that had all too long been ignored.

In society today there are still many cultural, artistic, and historical influences that originated from the Native Americans. We continue to reflect on the Nation's Native American History through books, museums, and those who are descendants may get to hear the narrative passed through generations.

Works Cited

Banks, Dennis J., and Richard Erdoes. Ojibwa Warrior: Dennis Banks and the Rise of the American Indian Movement. University of Oklahoma: Norman, 2004.

"Battle of the Little Bighorn, 1876." 1997.< http://www.eyewitnesstohistory.com>

Brown, Dee. Bury My Heart at Wounded Knee: An Indian History of the American West. New York: Holt, 1970.

"Crazy Horse." Oxford Family Encyclopedia. 1st ed. 1997.

Flood, Renee Sansom. Lost Bird of Wounded Knee: Spirit of the Lakota. New York: Da Capo Press, 1998.

"Massacre At Wounded Knee, 1890."1998<http://www.eyewitnesstohistory.com>.

Moss, George Donelson. Moving On: The American People Since 1945. Upper Saddle River: Pearson Prentice Hall, 2005

Peltier, Leonard, and Harvey Arden ed. <u>Prison Writings: My Life Is My Sun Dance</u>. New York: Crazy Horse, 1999.

"Trail of Tears." <http://ngeorgia.com/history/nghistt.html.>

ABOUT THE AUTHOR:

Kelcey grew up in the Northwest hunting, fishing, doing the cattle drive and being her own person.

She served in the United States Air Force alongside her little Brother as he served in the Marine Corps.

Kelcey went to college and attained an AA in Paralegal Studies then earned a BA in Psychology from AMU.

Today she works as a Paralegal, is a full time Mom to her Son, two Terriers-Jack Russell & Scottish. She still loves to fish in remembrance of her father and continues to enjoy the outdoors of the Pacific Northwest - hiking, camping, kayaking and skiing.

If you would like to make additional purchases as keepsakes or gifts, please visit my website at AmericanInjustice.net

*Thank you,
Kelcey*

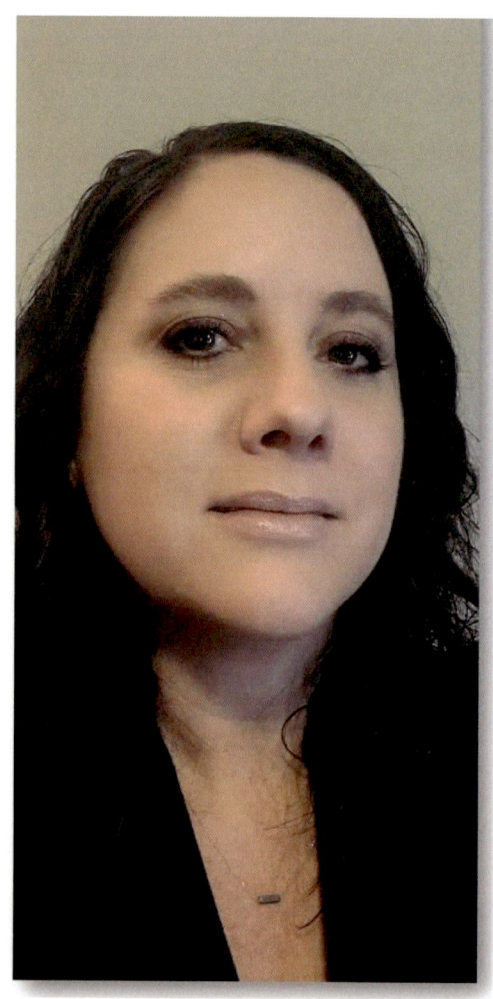

www.ingramcontent.com/pod-product-compliance
Lightning Source LLC
Chambersburg PA
CBRC092341290426
44109CB00011B/183